You

TOO

Can

Prosper

Tom Tompkins

Copyright 2017 Tom Tompkins

You TOO Can Prosper
ISBN 13: 978-1546378389
ISBN 10: 1546378383
Copyright © 2017 Lifetime Visionary

Published by Lifetime Visionary
lifetimevisionary.com

Reader Reviews

"What if your life could look different? What if the God of the Universe is trying to get your attention; to bring you into a new reality? In his new book, You Too Can Prosper, author Tom Tompkins unpacks these questions and more as he reveals God's heart for his children to prosper. Be prepared as you read Tompkins' new book to receive insight, practical solutions, and inspirational stories to take your life and your finances to the next level. Get ready - abundance is knocking at your door!"

Lucas Miles,
Author of Good God: The One We
Want To Believe In But Are
Afraid To Embrace.

YOU Too Can Prosper by Tom Tompkins. A roughly 113-page book which is soon to be out and available for you on Amazon.com! "The type of knowledge you possess will determine what you do and what you do not do in life." If you want to stay in the same old mundane 8-5 job and never prosper any more than what your current job can bring you, then this book is *not* for you. However, if you want to become more financially successful and gain to the point that you can live on the 3rd tier income, which means you may even get to take that much-needed vacation, then you will definitely want to read this book and pay attention to every page!

Whether you need to understand how to find direction to get started or need some guidance and encouragement on your already-started journey, this book will help you. It is never too late to change what you are doing. As Tom says, "I do not reveal this information to discourage you, but rather to bring comfort in knowing that it is not too late to change what is believed and ultimately what is experienced." So, rather than stay in your ordinary, day to day, dull, and routine life, start a change now that will bring you a smile where you can look back and be happy in a year from now, that you did start just by reading this short and simple, but very powerful book, *"YOU Too Can Prosper!"*

Faye Hanshew
Founder and CEO
Inspired Creations Publishing
Company LLC

Tom's book, You Too Can Prosper, has some life-changing nuggets that I believe will help launch many people into pursuing their God-given, big dreams as they learn throughout this powerful book that God is a Good Father who loves to see His children succeeding in life. I love the first sentence that starts the book off, "Nothing excites a parent more that seeing their child succeed." He makes it clear that this is no different with God related to His children. As you read this book, I believe you will learn not to settle for less than God's best and how to, as Tom puts it, "Chase after your dreams." I highly recommend this uplifting and encouraging book.

Nichole Marbach
Nichole Marbach Ministries

Excellent tool to begin your journey towards financial freedom to live a life of service towards others and the Lord. It is the initial shake one needs to wake up from a matrix world of routine and unfulfillment - unknowingly being a slave of money - to a life of prosperity with a purpose. You TOO can Prosper is the spark that will challenge your current state and lead you to seek answers towards your God ordained destiny.

Joyner Briceño
Joyner Briceno Ministries

"You TOO Can Prosper" is an encouraging and quick read. It's like getting to sit down with Tom Tompkins and have a fantastic discussion about his experiences and what it means biblically to prosper. There are numerous helpful suggestions throughout the book to kick start a change of thinking that produces the fruit of prosperity. Beginning with the desire and belief that prosperity is part of God's will for your life and that God loves you enough to offer direction to walk in

His prosperity. Tom Tompkins offers the basic principles of stepping out of the just enough into prosperity through asking God the questions that show you how to move forward in this area. "There are many paths available for wealth building" and investing in this book is a great place to start on your journey.

Rob and Lesa Statham

In You Too Can Prosper, my friend Tom Tompkins hits a grand slam! Profound wisdom written in bite size, simple strategies to help all of us begin to implement in our lives. I believe at my core that you and everyone that reads this writing by Tom will be better off for it. I believe that You TOO Can Prosper will put you on the path to discover your God given gifts, talents and will help you win like never before. Go Big because Yes - You TOO Can Prosper!

James Wood – The Disruptive Preacher

A practical view of biblical principles

Tom Tompkins approaches this sometimes-controversial subject of finances with boldness and assurance that God's will is to see us prosper. His advice is relayed in a simple, easy to understand format.

What may seem like a too good to be true dream for some, becomes amazingly reachable as they contemplate Tom's advice and encouragement mixed with God's strength and power.

This book could open so many doors for anyone wanting to move from a place of lack to a place of prosperity. If you're desiring to change and willing to work the plan in Tom's book, you too will prosper.

Linda Young,
Author of God Glasses – Change Your Vision For Life

This book is something I suggest everyone read. It is very practical and easy to understand yet loaded with information, perspectives and insights you possibly may have never thought of. I know I didn't. Tom was able to encapsulate what I believe prosperity really looks like, and give ideas and ways of not only attaining prosperity but living a continual life of being prosperous not only in finances, but every area of your life. I believe the reader of this book will be blessed with a new or better mindset to live a blessed and prosperous life that God has wanted for us the walk from the beginning.

Pastor Sherry Farmer. The Open Door Fellowship in Sapulpa Oklahoma

Acknowledgements

I would like to thank the following people who have had a positive impact on my life:

Heloise Tompkins

Tommy Tompkins

Pastor Timothy Carscadden

Andrew Wommack

Paul Milligan

Billy Epperhart

Rob and Lesa Statham

This list of amazing people have stood by me when I have been at my worst and when I have been at my best. Each has poured into me and continue to pour into me from a multitude of angles. Thank you for believing in me always. I appreciate, love and cherish each of you!

Special Thanks

Faye Hanshew
inspiredcreationspublishing.com
Thank you, Faye, for editing this book
and the time, effort and energy you put
into making this book a successful
reality.

Paul Milligan - I will never forget the first
time I heard you speak during 2006. Little
did I know that God was using you to set
me on a journey that would lead to
learning more about business and
leadership within a few years that,
without you, would have likely never
fully materialized in a lifetime.

Billy Epperhart – billyepperhart.com I
will never forget the many times you said,
"Don't give up, I am praying for you!"
Not only have you poured into my life in
business, real estate and leadership, but
you have motivated me with tremendous
encouragement.

Andrew Wommack – awmi.net Andrew, you have poured into my life by revealing to me who God really is. Not only have your poured into my life through your own teaching but through Charis Bible College and the many doors that opened to me by attending CBC and Charis Business School. Thank you!

Contents

Introduction XVIII

Chapter 1 The Will of God and Prosperity 1

Chapter 2 How to Find Direction . . . 9

Chapter 3 Where Are You Now? . . .19

Chapter 4 God Is in The Road Construction Business 29

Chapter 5 The Three Tiers of Income 37

Chapter 6 The Roadblock of Blind Faith 45

Chapter 7 Education Begins but Does Not End 55

Chapter 8 Be Encouraged 67

Chapter 9 How to Move Forward Based on What You Have Read . . . 77

Conclusion 85

Introduction

It is often said, "Knowledge is power." While this statement is true, there are two types of knowledge: right knowledge and wrong knowledge. It is possible to possess both right and wrong knowledge at the same time. The type of knowledge possessed is what determines the type of beliefs formed. The type of beliefs formed will determine how one's life looks as well as how the experiences of life are filtered, thus creating additional knowledge and beliefs (right or wrong).

The type of knowledge you possess will determine what you do and do not experience in life. Yes, it is possible to suddenly come into a large amount of money, also known as a windfall. A windfall is best described as an experience of receiving an unexpected increase, specifically related to finances.

You see, just because a person has a lot of money in the bank does not mean they know what to do with that money to allow the money to work for them, bringing increase. When all is said and done, the ultimate results are based on right or wrong knowledge.

I do not reveal this information to discourage you, but rather to bring comfort in knowing that it is not too late to change what you believe.

Throughout the pages of this book, I will deal with dispelling wrong beliefs and rumors about God, His will, and His ways. I will reveal how to prosper and why it is God's will for every person to flourish in all areas of life.

My prayer for you, the reader, is that God will use this book to answer questions you may have, questions you did not know you had, shine a light on His plan for your life and bring about hope in an area that seems impossible to change for the better.

Chapter 1
The Will of God and Prosperity

"Beloved, I pray that you may prosper in all things and be in health, just as your soul prospers."

3 John 2

Nothing excites a parent more than seeing their child succeed. No wonder so many people proudly display bumper stickers on their vehicle with words such as "My child is an honor student." They are proud of their child and happy to see good things taking place in his or her life. A good parent always wants to see their child succeed, have as few problems as possible and ultimately win in life.

In this example, the reason a parent wants to see only good things happen to their child is that God created each of us in His image. Not only does this reality apply from parent to child but also spouse to spouse and friend to friend.

Then God said, "Let Us make man in Our image, according to Our likeness."

Genesis 1:26

Having been created in God's image is not only based on outer traits but also inner desires. No wonder it is natural to resist experiences that create lack such as poverty and sickness. Nobody actively seeks to be poor.

Yes, out of a lack of understanding of God and His true nature, some have taken a vow of poverty, but where in the Bible is such an act accurately spelled out? Such a thing was most certainly not seen in the life of Jesus.

"For you know the grace of our Lord Jesus Christ, that though He was rich, yet for your sakes He became poor, that you through His poverty might become rich."

2 Corinthians 8:9

Some believe Jesus was poor, but where in scripture is such information accurately displayed? After all, from His birth, Jesus had much in the way of riches and resources such as gold frankincense and myrrh per the words of Matthew 2:11. There is much additional biblical information that details Jesus' wealth in the Bible, but I will allow you to research such information on your own. Yes, Jesus did "become" poor so that we may become rich. For Jesus to become poor, He had to move from being rich to being poor. This represents not only forgiveness of sins, but also the many additional benefits of salvation such as healing, soundness of mind and yes, financial prosperity.

To defend the belief that Jesus wants people to have little to nothing, many will bring up the story of the rich young ruler. One can see this story via the words of Matthew, (Matthew 19:16-22), Mark (10:17-22), and Luke (Luke 18:18-30). However, there is more to the story of the rich young ruler than often considered.

I often teach on what I call the 360-degree view. The 360-degree view allows one to see things from every possible angle whether from above, ground level, below or circling around. Many years ago, I learned the importance of looking at things from multiple angles by washing my car. If I washed my car, I could stand at the front of the car and look down the side of the car, not seeing anything, other than what appeared to be a clean car with no damage. However, if I walked to the back of the car, I would often see a small dent or ding that was visible due to a different point of view, depending on how the light was shining on the car. The point is this: it is important to view everything from all possible angles to avoid missing what could be hidden while looking from only one or two angles.

When applying this logic to the story of the rich young ruler, I want you to consider an important reality. None of us know what would have ultimately taken place had he submitted to the instruction of Jesus.

How many times have you heard a testimony in which a person was struggling financially, yet they gave all they had at church one day and received a tremendous blessing later that day or shortly after? I have heard many testimonies along these lines. It does happen! Yet, there is a problem.

The problem comes when others who are struggling in the area of finances hear such testimonies and think to themselves, "God is no respecter of persons. If He did it for them, He will do it for me!" They proceed to give all they have but end up suffering for weeks to come after doing so. What happened? The answer is found in following the instruction of God.

God told one person to give all they had, but He did not tell the person who heard about the results to do so. They did so based on leaning on their own understanding as opposed to trusting in the Lord and leaning *not* on their own natural and human understanding (Proverbs 3:5-6).

Had the rich young ruler simply followed the instruction of Jesus, he would have wound up with much more than he gave away.

"So Jesus answered and said, "Assuredly, I say to you, there is no one who has left house or brothers or sisters or father or mother or wife[a] or children or lands, for My sake and the gospel's, 30 who shall not receive a hundredfold now in this time—houses and brothers and sisters and mothers and children and lands, with persecutions—and in the age to come, eternal life."

Mark 10:29-30

Jesus was trying to position the rich young ruler to receive a one-hundred-fold return on what he was being instructed to give away. This is the reality and the will of God when it comes to prosperity and the creation of wealth.

Such a reality begins with right knowledge. When it comes to prosperity and being in health just as your soul prospers, it is important to understand what makes up the soul of man. The soul is comprised of the mind, will and emotions. If satan can convince a person that God does not want them to prosper, such beliefs will have a negative impact on the mind, will, and emotions of that person. No wonder those who struggle financially struggle to sleep, are sick and ultimately stressed out. Instinctively, each of us resists poverty, sickness and all additional forms of lack. We do so because God did not design us to embrace or embody such things.

Yes, God wants you to prosper and come to a place of being able to build wealth. After all, He has already placed such power on the inside of you.

"And you shall remember the LORD your God, for it is He who gives you power to get wealth, that He may establish His covenant which He swore to your fathers, as it is this day."

Deuteronomy 8:18

God has already given you the power to get wealth. The ability to walk in this power is based on what type of knowledge you are walking in (right or wrong).

Chapter 2
How to Find Direction

"You do not have because you do not ask."

James 4:2

God is not in the business of withholding important and necessary information from anyone. However, it is important to consider who God truly is and how He truly works. This information is plainly seen via two verses of scripture.

"God is love"

1 John 4:8

"Love doesn't force itself on others." *(Message Bible)*

1 Corinthians 13:5

I used to wonder why the description of love is seen via the words of 1

Corinthians 13:4-8 but come before the words, "God is love" seen in 1 John chapter four. But then I realized one must know what the description of love is before they can know that the description of love describes God.

The reason I bring this information to light is based on the fact that God does not force anything on anyone. Yes, there are times when God speaks to each of us, but we do not always realize it is God who is speaking or we may question whether it is Him or not.

You may not believe you hear or recognize God's voice. Please allow me to reveal to you how easily you hear His voice.

God has many names as seen via the Bible. Some of the names of God include the following: Abba Father, El Shaddai, Elohim, Yahweh and God's most commonly referred to name, Something.

Yes, God is often referred to as, Something, more often than any other name. Have you ever heard someone say, "Something told me"? You have likely uttered these words out of your mouth concerning something you did or wish you had done. As simple as this point is, it proves the reality that you hear God's voice.

"However, when He, the Spirit of truth, has come, He will guide you into all truth; for He will not speak on His own authority, but whatever He hears He will speak; and He will tell you things to come."

John 16:13

"My sheep hear My voice"

John 10:27

The words of John 16:13 reveal why many often say, "Something told me". God is always speaking to us about events to come, even warning of events to come to keep us out of trouble if at all possible. There is much to be said concerning this subject, but my point is this: you hear God's voice even if you do not recognize what is taking place. I will not go into an in-depth teaching concerning this subject, but I simply want to encourage you to know that you are fully capable of hearing His voice and already do.

A common problem throughout all of life is found in the struggle of finding direction. If you knew that you could easily find direction, would you take advantage of the avenues through which you could do so? What if you knew you could get answers to your questions? What about questions about money, making a living and creating wealth? What would you do if you knew such things were only one question away? With God, this is a present reality for each of us at this very moment.

Personally, I keep a journal in which I often have what I call Q & A with God. I will ask God a question and then allow Him to give me the answer to the question. I always write the question I ask and the response given from God. I will ask questions as simple as, "God, what do you want to tell me?" or "God, what are you positioning me for?" When I am asking God a question about a major, pressing or serious situation in my life, I am as specific as I can be. I may ask a question such as, "God, why did that business deal fall through?" or "Why does it seem like what you are speaking to me is not coming to pass at this time?"

However, what should you do if you are not sure what question or questions to ask God? There is a simple solution to such a problem. If you do not know what question to ask God, ask God what question or questions He wants you to ask. He will give you the questions He wants you to ask and also give you the answer to those questions.

To what questions are you seeking answers? Why not write those questions down whether or paper on a computer screen, leaving enough room for the answer God gives you? It may seem odd at first, but after a period of time, you will go back and read those questions and answers, discovering that the very answers God gave you are materializing in your life at the very moment in which you are reading over them.

When I began this practice, I wondered if I was truly hearing from God. You may do the same thing. I have had several events take place in which I have been praying for others and would receive a word for the person for whom I was praying. The word would be right on, but I have struggled to know that I am hearing from God for myself confidently. I have had three specific events in which God proved to me that I am hearing from Him.

The first confirmation came at the ministry of a friend of mine, Cecil Paxton. While living in Colorado, I always enjoyed going to his prayer ministry training sessions to see what nuggets I could learn; never leaving disappointed.

A common practice during these meetings involved Cecil asking those in attendance to find someone they did not know to pray with them. He would encourage us to pray and then share anything we received for the person for whom we were praying. One particular Friday night, I wound up praying with a man from Colorado Springs by the name of Brad. The two of us had not met before, so we knew nothing of one another. What happened next was amazing.

After Brad prayed for a minute or so he began to share with me what God had shown him. He said, "God wants you to know that you are truly hearing His voice. You do not need to doubt that you are hearing from God." I was floored!

The second event was when my friend, Marcus, had a tremendous word for me. During this word from the Lord that came through the mouth of Marcus, he said, "You have often questioned if the desires you have are of God. God wants you to know that those desires are from Him and of Him!"

Once again, I was floored as my friend, Marcus, had no idea of what was taking place in my life and the fact that I was questioning God if the things I was praying for were of Him along with questioning whether I heard His voice or my own voice. Many of you will face the same lie from the devil, but do not worry. Not only can you ask God what questions He wants you to ask Him, but you are also able to ask Him to confirm that you are truly hearing from Him. I cannot say how He may reveal this to you, but I can assure you that He will be happy to show you in the way that He knows is best. Keep in mind, the sign, if you want to call it that, may not come immediately but it will come.

The third experience came directly from God. I was at the grocery store, simply minding my own business. I turned the corner off the aisle I had been on and saw a lady slowly pushing her shopping cart along. She appeared to be looking for something. As soon as I saw her, *Something* told me to tell her God loved her. I instantly thought to myself, "Was that God or was that just my voice telling me to do that?" As soon as I had this thought I heard God say, "If you knew it was me and you did not have to rely on your power, but instead rely on my power, would you be willing to go tell that lady I love her?" Of course, I said, "Yes!" So, I eased up beside this lady, a total stranger and said, "Hi! I just wanted to tell you that God loves you and is pleased with you just as you are."

Her initial response was, "Well, I try to be a good person." At that very moment, I thought to myself, "It must not have been God, but you can't go wrong with telling someone God loves them." But then she began to get emotional and cry. What she said next told the tale and brought me into the realm of reality concerning the situation.

"I have had a hard time since this past September because that is when my mom passed away."

I knew then that I had truly heard from God and was glad that I not only listened but followed His instruction. I prayed for this lady before moving on. She was very touched by the situation. As I walked away, this total stranger said, "I love you." It was nothing odd. Only a heartfelt gratitude. It made my day! I walked away and turned onto an aisle a few feet away. As soon as I made the turn onto the aisle I heard God say, "Now do you believe you hear my voice clearly?"

Are there times when I still wonder? Yes, but I do know that God told me to always move forward with whatever I believe He has told me to do even when I am not sure if it was His voice. Keep in mind, doing such a thing is no danger when you know the Word of God and the reality that God will not violate His Word.

I have written all of this information to encourage you to not worry about whether or not you are truly hearing from God. Ask for confirmation if needed, but move forward with what you believe He is telling you as quickly as possible.

Chapter 3
Where Are You Now?

I want you to stop for a minute (or more if needed) and ask yourself a question. The question I want you to ask yourself is, "Am I truly happy with where I am in life at this very moment?"

What was your answer? If you are honest with yourself, you may be living well, paying your bills and enjoying a few good times in life, but what would happen if you lost your current source of income? How would the experience effect you? How long could you survive? Some may say, "I know there is more, but I have no idea how to get to the point of more." On the other hand, many people may say, "I can't afford a scraper to scrape by."

Most people rely a job as their primary or singular source of income.

Additionally, those who have jobs are those who commonly struggle financially, living paycheck to paycheck. Others may have a little more than enough but are up to their ankles in debt and in head first. Those who often appear to have the most are struggling to pay their bills to maintain the look of being wealthy.

Where do you fit? I am not trying to bring condemnation on anyone. I simply want you to look at your current situation to determine if you are happy or not. If you lost your job or your business closed, how long could you maintain your current lifestyle? These are questions that must be addressed to move toward building wealth. This is due to the fact that wealth is not built from earning a paycheck or having a job. Yes, there is a tremendous difference between earning a paycheck and having an income. I will discuss this subject further in chapter five when I unpack the three tiers of income.

So, where are you right now? What does your financial snapshot look like?

Are you pleased with your financial snapshot? Your financial snapshot is the overall view of your assets and liabilities.

Many spend their careers using the earn and save method. This practice involves saving a given amount of money from each paycheck to create a nest egg, as it is commonly known, to prepare for retirement. May I present to you the reality that the earn and save method simply does not bring any true benefit? This information may come as a shock so please allow me to explain.

When it comes to retirement and living off the nest egg that was created using the earn and save method, a rather unpleasant experience takes place. Money that has already been taxed once, when earned on the job, will continue to be taxed during retirement years. Additionally, the nest egg begins to shrink while being used to cover living expenses as well as vacations or the occasional unexpected expense. After decades of saving to retire, living frugally and making regular sacrifices, a new stress rears its ugly head. This is the stress that comes with money leaving, but not returning.

Yes, one may have retirement and social security, but after developing the habit of earning and saving, many fall into fear because they want to save as much as possible. Not only does stress come from this manner of living, but also from not being able to simply enjoy life by traveling, having a hobby or simply knowing that there is money coming in on a regular basis without one having to work for it. Retirement income may come in but is often rather small, forcing the majority to live on a fixed income.

Have you ever known a person who developed health problems or died shortly after retiring? What I have described is one of the primary reason for such an experience.

Where are you at this point in the area of finances? Based on what I have discussed in this chapter, you should know the answer to this question. You may have a supposed safe, secure job. However, I can say beyond a shadow of a doubt that there is no such thing as a safe, secure job. Such a thing may have existed during the industrial age, a time when people were much more patient, and technology was not readily available to replace people as it is today during the information age. Please allow me to share a couple of stories that reveal the harsh reality of being an employee.

A relative of mine once had a great job. A personal friend of many years had given him an incredible opportunity to work as the plant manager at a local company. The pay way great. In fact, he was able to build a stunning new home of 3600 square feet on waterfront property. The home was on a street that was affectionately known as millionaire's row.

After having been at this particular company for a few years, I would occasionally hear my relative say, "I keep having a feeling that I am going to lose my job." A year or so later, he went to lunch with a six-figure salary, only to return from lunch with no salary at all. Yes, he lost his job in an instant. Try as he may, there was nothing he could do to remedy the situation. He was forced to sell the beautiful home he and his wife had built one year prior to this experience.

Personally, I have a story of my own to share. At one time, there was a General Motors plant in my hometown of Shreveport, La. I had been in business for ten years at this time, but things had been challenging and inconsistent. When all was said and done, I simply did not know how to run a successful business at that point in time. Had I only known then what I know now! Famous last words, right?

I had a good friend who worked at the GM plant who once mentioned to me that the plant would hire summer vacation replacement help to allow regular employees to go on vacation. The pay was great and there was commonly a strong opportunity of being hired full time. I was fortunate enough to be chosen as one of the summer vacation replacement hires. I never had a difficult job because I was classified a temporary, which meant seniority was not an issue, I wound up with two of the highest positions within the entire plant! That is the favor of God! I worked many hours, but the work was easy. My net income for 60 total days of work was roughly $20,000. Not too bad for an employee.

At the time, I was praying for full time employment, however, this did not work out. I was not happy with the outcome. I remember a particular day when I was leaving the plant location. I remember it so well that I could take you to the spot where I was sitting in my car and show you where I was. I can still see it as if I am sitting in my car at that spot right this second.

At that moment, I considered that the plant may close one day and I would be grateful for having not been hired fulltime. Keep in mind, the summer vacation replacement workers from the previous year to my tenure had been hired full time and were working at the plant alongside me and others in my group. A few years later, GM ran into enormous financial problems and was forced to close several of its plants across the country. The closures included the Shreveport plant which had been in operation since the early 1980s.

Keep in mind, the jobs at the plant had a starting pay of roughly $26.00 per hour, yet the average job in Shreveport pays $10.00 per hour. Had I been hired, I would have likely taken full advantage of the ability to borrow money and have many toys. At that point in time, I did not understand money as I do today. The group of vacation replacement workers hired the year prior to my hiring were given a $25,000 severance package, but not given the option to transfer to another plant. I can guarantee you that most of those people were in a tough place as they likely had incurred much debt due to a good salary.

Such a salary is difficult to find in the Shreveport area for many. On a side note, my relative who lost the six-figure job would often see those who had been laid off from GM come to his place of employment seeking a job. After having worked at GM for what amounted to seventy-five percent of the starting salary (roughly $19.00 per hour), they would begin working at the company where my relative was working for less than $9.00 per hour! What a harsh reality.

Sadly, such scenarios are a common experience for many: going from job to job or losing a job and finding it difficult to find a job of equal pay for what can amount to long periods of time. During such times, the bills continue to come in and are more difficult to pay.

A friend of mine lost a job that paid $50,000 per year. While not a large amount of money, her salary was beneficial to she and her family. As of the time in which I am writing this book, she is still seeking a job of similar pay after eight months but is currently working for $9.00 per hour.

Keep in mind; I am not saying it is wrong to be an employee. What I am saying is that one must be prepared for the potential challenges that could come from being an employee. If you lose your job today, when will you run out of money? How long will your funds last? How will things work after retirement? What options are available to a person who may want to continue working at their job, yet begin building wealth?

During the course of the rest of this book, I will answer such questions among others.

Chapter 4
God Is in The Road Construction Business

Many of the points I made in chapter three are likely identifiable to some readers based on experience. At the very least, I hope I was able to help you see things differently and consider some of the potentials of the changes you may want to make. What does the future hold? Is it possible to make decisions today that will have a positive effect on tomorrow and beyond?

Based on the information I discussed in chapter three, you may realize that you are not pleased with your current financial situation. If so, what are your options? How do you begin the trek of moving from where you currently are to where you want to be? Better yet, what about moving from where you are to where God wants you to be? Remember, it is God's will for you to walk in prosperity (3 John 2). Your greatest plans for your life cannot compare to God's plans for your life.

"God can do anything, you know—far more than you could ever imagine or guess or request in your wildest dreams! He does it not by pushing us around but by working within us, his Spirit deeply and gently within us." (Message Bible)

Ephesians 3:20-21

The power that works within us is nothing more than placing faith in God and His promises. It is a natural step of trusting in God and not leaning on our natural understanding.

"Trust GOD from the bottom of your heart;

don't try to figure out everything on your own. Listen for GOD's voice in everything you do, everywhere you go;

he's the one who will keep you on track.

Don't assume that you know it all."
(Message Bible)

Proverbs 3:5-6

When you lean on your understanding or the understanding of others, what might make sense in the natural is not what makes sense to God. When the Bible says, "God's ways are higher than our ways" via the words of Isaiah 55:9, it does not mean God will allow or cause tragedy or difficult times in your life for any number of reasons. God simply does not work that way. God's ways are higher because His plans are so grand for each of us that some of us are not ready to hear those plans at this point. His plans are the type that many will believe impossible or could not possibly be from God. We are the ones who need to come up to the high altitude of God's plans and desires.

Personally, God recently spoke to me and said, "I want you to believe for a net income of $30,000 per week." Such

31

information challenges me which is okay to admit. There is nothing wrong with admitting that we may not be at a place from which we can believe for something that big. However, God also told me that $30,000 per week in net income is not even close to what He untimely desire for me! That is astonishing!

I don't bring this information up to toot my own horn but to simply make a point. If God has such desires for us, we need only rely on Him to lead the way and show us how to move from where we are to where He wants us to be. It won't happen overnight, but each of us can take a step that will allow us to begin making forward progress.

As you read in an earlier chapter, you know I am passionate about teaching others to ask God questions and allow Him to give answers. Over the last couple of years, I have discovered something that God has said to me many times.

The answer I am referring to is, "I just want you to trust me." For the longest time, I became annoyed with this. I would ask God a question and say, "Please don't tell me to trust you." In my mind, this meant there was going to be yet another delay in receiving the answer to my prayers. However, in time, I discovered why He would ask me to trust Him. It now makes perfect sense and has transformed my life.

For many years, I struggled with impatience, which led to a large amount of frustration through many areas of my life. I was leaning on my understanding. When God said, "Trust me" He was not trying to annoy me nor was He trying to tell me that the answers to my prayers were far away. He was trying to tell me that His ways are higher than my ways and if I would simply listen to Him and follow His instructions, things would work much better than they would otherwise.

How do you go about changing the way you think based on using verses of scripture found in the Bible? Believe it or not, the process isn't difficult. There may be varying amounts of time it takes to see the change take place, but no matter what the timeframe may be, it Is worth the time and ultimate results.

It is important to find a couple of verses of scripture such as Proverbs 3:5-6 and Ephesians 3:20. I highly recommend taking as much time as needed, whether it is a couple of days, weeks or even months to meditate on verses such as these or others that apply to any challenge you need to overcome. Read them several times per day. In time, you will memorize them, and they will become an instant reaction when facing a given situation that may have caused anger or fear in the past, which has most certainly been my experience.

Think of it this way: when you are going through a difficult time or even a great time, such experiences dominate your thoughts. No matter what you are doing, you think about those things when eating, driving, working and sleeping. You are already an expert in meditation. I am not talking about anything weird. The word meditate is defined as meaning, to engage in contemplation or reflection (Source – Merriam - Webster). You already know how to meditate. Why not apply your skills to meditating on scripture? Such a practice is one method that God can use to take you from where you are to where He wants you to be.

When all is said and done, there is no age barrier, skin color barrier, gender barrier or any additional barrier to stop you from moving from where you are to a much better place. It is simply a matter of changing what you believe.

Chapter 5
The Three Tiers of Income

Everybody is living from at least one of the three tiers of income. Some people are living from two of the three tiers and possibly all three. What are the three tiers of income?

Tier 1 – money that is earned. This is commonly from a job/working as an employee.

Tier 2 – Money working for you. This is commonly seen by having employees working for you within a business.

Tier 3 – Money that works without your having to be present. Tier 3 income encompasses several avenues such as intellectual properties, rental properties or investing money in business ventures.

Tier 1 is where most people live. Tier 1 income comes from being an employee or being self-employed. Being self-employed is the experience of working alone and handling all jobs required to operate with your two hands. Self-employment is also known as creating a job for yourself. Tier 1 income is risky as employment can end any day for any number of reasons. Self-employment is also risky as being a one person show often leads to burnout within a given period of time. The amount of money earned on tier 1 can vary and in some cases, could be higher than what a person living in tier 2 is earning. However, one of the major drawbacks to being an employee is that money is taken from your paycheck before you see it via taxes and other areas of withholding.

An important point to consider is one of the harshest realities of tier 1. What I am referring to is income taxes. There are variations of how much tax is paid by an employee depending on a number of variables. I won't take the time to get into what these are, but keep in mind, taxes are likely not all that come off your paycheck before you see it. Health insurance and a contribution to a 401K are examples of potential deductions that could take money from your paycheck before you receive it.

Tier 2 is commonly where the business owner is found. There is a difference between being self-employed and being a business owner. The business owner has a staff of people handling most daily tasks, taking the load of doing everything with the same pair of hands which could ultimately lead to burnout among additional problems, which is also known as having money working for you.

If the business owner understands how to structure earnings or has an accountant who understands such a thing, they can take advantage of tax laws that allow them to avoid paying the high-income taxes of someone who is living on tier 1. There are tax advantages available on tier 2 that are not available on tier 1.

Tier 3 is most certainly the best place to live. Tier 3 is where wealth is created. As mentioned earlier, this is where money works without you. There are several avenues from which this can take place from royalties from book sales, CD sales, rental properties or investments in the stock market.

Keep in mind, unless you were born into a wealthy family, you will likely begin working on tier 1 before moving on to tier 2 or 3. It is possible to move from tier 1 to tier 3 or have multiple sources of income coming from more than one of the three tiers. Obviously, tier 3 is the best place to live, but how does a person move from tier 1 to tier 2 and eventually to tier 3?

The first step involves getting out of debt, which may seem like a daunting task, but I am about to show you a simple formula that will allow you pay off all debt, including your vehicles and home within a one to seven-year period.

This process begins with finding some extra money, the money you likely did not know you had available. Keep in mind, this process is likely to involve some sacrifice, but it will be worth relieving yourself of a load of debt. Where is this extra money? Stop to consider something you are spending money on regularly that you simply do not need or can live without for a time. Whether you reduce the amount of money you spend at the coffee shop several times per week or cut trips to the coffee shop out altogether, you have already found extra money to put toward getting out of debt. What about ending the country club membership or turning off the cable or satellite? Yes, it is a sacrifice, but it is worth it.

Not only will you find yourself with extra money to begin the process of paying off all debt, but you could also have extra time to study on the subject of money or read biographies and so on. There are many advantages.

So, let's say you came up with an extra $50.00 to put toward paying off all debt, which may seem like a small amount to begin with. But over time it will grow tremendously depending on how much debt you have to pay off. Additionally, once all debt has been paid off, you will have a large amount of money to apply toward creating wealth and moving toward tier 2 and eventually tier 3 income!

The process works by starting with the smallest debt. Let's say it is a credit card with a minimum payment of $17.99 per month. When you apply the $50.00 you came up with, the new monthly payment becomes $67.99. This process adds tremendously to the principle which automatically kills/reduces the interest, allowing the credit card to be paid off quickly as opposed to taking many additional years. Once the credit card is paid off in full, you will have $67.99 to apply to the next debt. Let's say the next debt after the credit card is a school loan with a minimum monthly payment of

$99.99. When the $67.99 is added, you are suddenly paying $166.98. By now I believe you see how this process works. Each time a debt is paid off, the amount applied from all previously paid off debts grows each time until making it to the final and largest debt. In many cases, the amount could be near or at five figures.

During the course of paying off all debt, it is important to begin researching and discovering how and where you will invest the extra money once you are debt free, which is how you will continue the process of creating wealth.

Finally, please allow me to caution you against what could be a tremendous mistake. On the way to paying off all debt, many are planning to treat themselves to a reward to celebrate the accomplishment of becoming debt free. Such a mistake could lead to going into debt all over again. It is okay to go out to eat or hold a party to celebrate but don't buy a new car or other expensive item with the extra money you now have. I highly recommend discovering the best way to use the money you end up with after all debt has been paid off for an investment or number of investments that will allow the money to work for you or without you.

There are many paths available for wealth building. It is up to you to ask God the questions that will allow Him to show you how to move forward in this area. You know how to go about doing this based on what we discussed in an earlier chapter.

Is there more to moving from tier 1 income to tier 2 and eventually to tier 3? Yes! Is it possible to move from tier 1 to tier 3? Yes! What is best for you and what are the steps to doing so? Ask God and allow Him to give you the answers, but also be sure to take the steps He gives you or you will never make progress.

Chapter 6
The Roadblock of Blind Faith

I once had a conversation with a friend about living by faith and living from miracle to miracle. Through the course of the conversation, I made mention of the fact that living from miracle to miracle is not God's best for any of us. I also made mention of the fact that seeking to live from miracle to miracle and believing that doing such a thing is living by faith is ultimately rooted in blind faith.

In essence, the difference between living from miracle to miracle as opposed to living in the blessings of God is much like the difference between assets and liabilities.

An asset is anything that puts money in your pocket.

A liability is anything that takes money out of your pocket.

The best way I can describe these two areas is to use a band-aid as an example. A band-aid is a temporary fix for a cut or scrape. However, over time, the adhesive on the band-aid will wear out, causing the band-aid to fall off, re-exposing the wound. Please allow me to explain further.

It may seem noble to live by faith and tie such a thing to living from miracle to miracle. Yes, faith is involved in receiving a miracle, but God has a better way.

First of all, let's look at what faith is. According to the words of Hebrews 11:1, faith is the substance of things hoped for, the evidence of things not seen. However, faith is not the substance of what you already have.

Secondly, let's consider the fact that faith is not needed for what you already have. Faith is needed when something is missing, lacking or not functioning as it should. Please understand, I am not saying faith is bad. I have needed faith at different times in my life, all of which involved some sort of crisis.

To simplify things, I will cut to the chase. Just as an asset is something that puts money in your pocket, alleviating a financial crisis or struggle, living in the blessings of God as opposed to living from miracle to miracle, alleviates the opportunity for living from struggle to struggle or crisis to crisis. Living in the blessings of God will remove the need for a miracle. Believe it or not, God did not create any of us to live in lack or from crisis to crisis. Ultimately, a crisis is a liability. A crisis may not take money out of your pocket on every occasion, but it does have the opportunity to remove peace from your life. For this reason, I compare living from crisis to crisis or miracle to miracle to living with liabilities.

Yes, it is possible to live in the blessings of God, but still, experience an occasional crisis just as it is possible to live with assets and liabilities at the same time.

Before we move on, let's look at a verse of Scripture, when misused as it commonly is, can bring about a crisis and an acceptance of living from miracle to miracle. The verse I wish to cover is Philippians 4:11. In this verse, in context with Philippians 4:12-13, the apostle Paul speaks of being content in all things. Many have understood this to mean that each of us should be satisfied no matter how good or bad things may be in our lives. In other words, we should accept things as they are at all times. However, this is not the point the apostle Paul was trying to make. The reality of these verses and their meaning is found in the meaning of the word, content, which means: to be calm and at peace in all situations.

The word content means to be calm, at peace and not worried no matter what is or is not going on, but it does not mean to accept things as they are. Doing so will create passivity and cause one to miss out on God's best.

"For the eyes of the LORD run to and fro throughout the whole earth, to show Himself strong on behalf of those whose heart is loyal to Him."

2 Chronicles 16:9

God's ways are higher and better than our ways (Isaiah 55:9) which means His standards are higher and better than our best. He always has more for each of us and does not desire to see us living in lack in any area of life (3 John 2).

Blind faith unknowingly embraces crisis and expects it to come, thinking, "It's okay! God will give me a miracle to get through." Whether it involves finances, health or any additional number of opportunities for miracles to take place. God wants to see you live in His blessings as opposed to needing a miracle. Yes, signs and wonders (miracles included) are great, but what would you rather experience? Needing a miracle to be healed of cancer or living cancer free? One method involves needing a miracle while the other involves simply living in the blessings of God. What would you rather experience, needing a miracle to eat and pay your bills or know that you can set up auto pay because you know the money is always available and you do not have to worry about it? One method involves needing a miracle while the other involves simply living in the blessings of God.

When the rubber meets the road, your experiences in these areas are based on what you believe (Proverbs 23:7). If you are not happy with the results you are experiencing, you may want to consider changing what you believe.

Blind faith may seem like a good thing until the blinders have been removed. For this reason the words of Deuteronomy 8:18 speak of the fact that God has given each of us the power to get wealth. Wealth

comes from living from third tier income
– money that works without you.

Stop and think about what we have
discussed in this chapter. Would you
rather live from miracle to miracle or
from blessing to blessing?

It is the thief, (satan) who comes to
steal, kill and destroy per the words of
John 10:10. If he cannot accomplish such
things in your life directly, he will try to
blind you with wrong beliefs. What would
you rather experience? The stress and
strain of not knowing for sure where your
next paycheck is coming from or when it
is coming or would you rather know your
paycheck is coming and you do not need
to think about it? God does not want you
to be stressed or concerned with finances.

Even if you have seen many regular
miracles and are not behind or stretched
in the area of finances, if there were a
better way to live, would you want to
know about it? How would you feel if you
woke up each morning and did not need
to consider where the next payment was

coming from for your home, car(s) or utility bills? What if the economy takes another dive and you can sit back and relax because God has already brought you to a place in which money is not an issue for you? How would such a reality change your life for the better?

Please allow me to make a radical statement: There is no place in the Bible in which Jesus told anyone to believe for money! I already addressed the story of the rich young ruler which means you cannot use his story to say God wants you or anyone else to give away everything you have and live with little to nothing. In all reality, there is no place throughout the Bible to accurately back up the belief that poverty is of God, is humbling or a blessing.

If you are not happy with your current level of income or your experience in the area of finances, I encourage you to start asking God questions and allowing Him to give you the answers that will allow you go from where you are to where He wants you to be.

Yes, you may face some crisis in life, but you do not have to live from crisis to crisis. What are you willing to believe for, are you willing to become dissatisfied with living outside of God's best? If you are struggling in the smallest place in the area of finances, I can guarantee you that God has a much better plan for you. Take a few minutes to have a time of Q & A with God to discover what the first step is to moving away from living from miracle to miracle (crisis to crisis) and begin living from blessing to blessing.

Chapter 7
Education Begins but Does Not End

According to current statistics, seventy percent of lottery winners or those who receive a large windfall file for bankruptcy or return to their former financial struggles within a few years of the experience. The timeframe in which this happens ranges from one to five years.

Have you ever thought that your problems would be over if you received a specific amount of money? I know there have been times in my life when this was the case. However, when I received the money I needed during those past times, typically via a miracle, it did not take long before I needed another miracle because I had not properly used the money I received. In some cases, the money a person may need in addition to what they already have has already been spent on bills before it ever reaches their bank account. Such a reality is a clear sign of the need for a financial education.

As I mentioned earlier, the example of a band-aid fits into the scenario that leads from sudden financial gain to a return to financial hardship. Without a change in the way a person thinks or understands something, such as money, the same problems will continue to exist, but are temporarily covered until the adhesive wears off or in this case, the money runs out.

Why is this such a common problem? The main reason is a lack of the changing of the way a person thinks. If a person comes into a large amount of money, their understanding of money and how it works does not instantly change. If that person is used to spending every penny they have, they will continue to do so no matter how much money they do or do not have.

For those who struggle financially, there is a common problem that comes up when extra money comes along. It is not uncommon to believe it is okay to splurge and buy something special or go out for a special time such as eating out at a nice restaurant or traveling. Keep in mind, I am not saying it is wrong to go out and have fun. After all, the stress and strain of financial struggle or lack often lead to the desire to do something special when the rare opportunity is available. A person who receives a windfall often loses everything quickly. The same mindset is in place no matter how little or how much money is available.

Financial education is ongoing for anyone who understands money and how to put it to work on their behalf. But how does a person who has never learned about money go about beginning the process of learning? For many who understand money, their education began in the home. They learned from their parents. Many, such as myself, did not learn much about the subject of money from our parents but have been able to learn contrary to prior experiences.

Yes, I learned how to save money from my parents, but I also learned how to spend. In fact, as is the case with many, learning to save was based on planning to spend. I knew how to save up to buy a particular item, but once I made the purchase, I had little to nothing left over. I was at or near zero. Saving with the intention of spending money on a liability is the opposite of building wealth. Yes, there is a need for a savings account or as some call it, an emergency fund. A proper financial education and the practice of building wealth will allow money to always be present for any emergency that may come along.

What I am ultimately speaking of is living from the third tier of income, which is where money works without you. Living from the third tier comes from proper financial education just as staying on the third tier of income is partially based on your financial education in the form of past, present, and future.

So, what if you are like me and did not learn much about money if anything from your parents? First of all, do not condemn your parents for not teaching you about money. For those of us who fall into this category, our parents could not teach us what they did not know. Thankfully, it is never too late to start learning no matter your age.

Here are a few methods that you could use to begin and continue learning about money and furthering your financial education.

- Reading books
- Audiobooks
- Attending financial seminars
- Free and paid online training
- Classes taught through your local Small Business Development Association
- Taking a wealthy person to lunch and asking them questions
- Watching biographies of those who are wealthy

- Asking God how to move from where you are to where He wants you to be

Please allow me to highlight some of the areas mentioned in the list which, by the way, is not a complete list, but rather a list of some of the easiest ways to learn about money, how it works and how to put it to work.

Classes taught through your local small business development association Many cities have a Small Business Development Association (SBDA). Although one of the primary objectives of the SBDA is to help business owners obtain funding for their venture, the SBDA also offers regular classes on a wide range of subjects including finances and how money works. All of the classes are taught by experienced professionals. Many classes are free or may cost a small amount to attend.

Taking a wealthy person to lunch and asking them questions Take a wealthy person to lunch and ask them as many questions as you possibly can. Of course, you need to be sure to pay for their meal which is an important factor in keeping the door open for future meetings. In addition, be sure to have a list of questions you want to ask before meeting for lunch. You will also want to be prepared for any questions you may be asked. If you cannot answer, do not worry. Do the best you can but keep in mind, the wealthy understand the need to be prepared. The more prepared you are before your first meeting, the better chance you will have a second meeting and beyond. Keep in mind, if you are going into business and need an investor, you may be talking to someone who is willing to step up and finance your venture!

Asking God how to move from where you are to where He wants you to be I covered this topic in an earlier chapter, but it most certainly bears repeating. No matter where you are or what you are doing, it is always important to ask God what He has to say about a given situation or venture. Remember, the more specific the questions you ask God, the more specific His answers will be to you. If you are not sure how to proceed, ask God what the first step is, but remember an important point.

God commonly gives each of us one step at a time. He wants us to trust Him and continue to trust Him. God commonly gives us one step at a time instead of several steps that may lead to our moving forward on our own without trusting God and seeking Him first in all we do (Proverbs 3:5-6 with Matthew 6:33).

Those are what I consider to be the three most important points on the list. I believe the rest are self-explanatory.

When all is said and done, your education in the area of finances is something that should begin, but not end. After all, the economy is constantly changing as are laws that relate to the economy and business. The more you know, the better of you will be. There are tax laws that allow entrepreneurs to save on taxes being paid. Yes, such things are legal and have been put in place by the government. What are they? You will need to further your education to find out! Did you really think I would make it that easy for you?

Before I end this chapter, I want to discuss one of the most common methods that people use to gain their financial education. In essence, I have already discussed this topic but will use different words. One of the most common and unhelpful practices for learning about money is attending the school of hard knocks. Some people seem to have chosen to become lifelong students.

Contrary to some popular Christian teaching, God never wants you to learn the hard way.

"Do not be like the horse or like the mule, Which have no understanding, Which must be harnessed with bit and bridle, Else they will not come near you."

Psalm 32:9

Are you familiar with how a bit works in the mouth of a horse or mule? In simplest terms, the bit provides direction for the animal. This process takes place via pain felt in the mouth of the animal. Somebody else may be able to give a better explanation, but I like to keep things as simple as possible.

When all is said and done, God does not want our paths to be directed through the pain. Pain is not meant to be your roadmap. This is one of the reasons why God has given us the Holy Spirit: To provide direction and tell us what is coming so we will know how to deal with things ahead of time (John 16:13).

God does not want any of us to attend a single class in the school of hard knocks, but if you are like me, you have attended several classes. I try to avoid such classes/experiences as often as possible.

The right education will aid in this area. No, there is not a perfect education, but learn as much as you can. Over time, you will learn enough to know right from wrong when continuing your education, allowing you to spit out the bones and chew on the meat.

I want to encourage you to continue your education today and beyond. You are already doing so by reading this book, but there are many additional resources that you will need to know about to understand money.

Chapter 8
Be Encouraged

- You cannot come up with a dream, goal or desire that is too big.
- If you can see yourself succeeding, you will succeed.
- If you have a dream, chase after it.
- If you fail, get up, dust yourself off and keep going.
- Never give up!
- Just because someone before you could not accomplish what it is you want to accomplish, does not mean you cannot succeed.
- You are a winner!
- You are a champion!
- Be the first and allow others to follow in your footsteps.
- Don't stop dreaming big!

"Now to Him who is able to [carry out His purpose and] do superabundantly more than all that we dare ask or think [infinitely beyond our greatest prayers, hopes, or dreams], according to His power that is at work within us." *(Amplified Bible)*

Ephesians 3:20

How is it possible to not be able to come up with a dream, goal or desire that is too big? The answer is found within the words of Ephesians 3:20. The plans of God for your life are greater than anything you could desire on your own. It is that simple! But for some, this is a complicated matter.

For many of us, our God-given imagination has been dormant since an early age. After all, Jesus Himself said we are to come to Him as a child or with childlike imagination and expectation via the words of Matthew 19:14.

If you were to ask a child what their expectations are for the future, they would likely tell you what they are going to be and what they are going to do. The explanation is likely to be detailed and thorough. Some might call such things, lofty. In many cases, over the course of time, such big dreams are brought into supposed reality by well-meaning family and friends who are ultimately killing the ability of the child, who will eventually become an adult, to use his imagination to begin the process of doing great things. It is important to remember this fact; Meaning well and being right do not always go hand in hand.

It is important to note, none of us can have something working in our lives that we cannot first see (imagine). The words of Proverbs 23:7 solidify this point.

"For as he thinks in his heart, so is he" (Amplified Bible)

Many may tell those around them what they are going to do such as starting a company that will make millions or they may speak of plans to peruse a multi-million-dollar idea. However, many will instantly give them every reason why they cannot succeed at accomplishing such a thing. Such action can kill creativity and destroy the use of imagination at any age although most adults do not use their imagination in a positive way, to begin with.

When I was growing up, I loved the sport of drag racing. I would race anything I could find from my bicycle to a go-cart.

Eventually, I came up with an idea to make my experience of pretending to be a race car driver as realistic as possible.

I would take a tape recorder to the races with me along with several cassette tapes, yes, I am dating myself, and record the sounds from the action of the races. I would then return home while racing my bicycle or go-cart and replay the tapes from the races. Eventually, I got my neighborhood friends involved as my pit crew and had a lot of fun pretending to race. At the age of 16, I began to race for real with a real race car. A cassette playing over a stereo in my backyard was no longer needed. I was amazed at how realistic the backyard racing had been when compared to the real thing. It was amazing!

When I was racing in the backyard of my parents' home, with the sounds of the races playing on cassette, I also saw myself winning every race I pretended to attend. I believe this was part of the reason why I was highly successful when it came to the real thing, winning not only races, but championships as well. My imagination had served me well.

Over the years, I have been told of what I was not capable of such as hearing that I was not college material or could not succeed in business for any number of reasons. Sure enough, I struggled my way through college and had struggles in business over the years as well. However, I was never told that I could not succeed in driving a race car. Some of my greatest success in life has been on the race track, but I do not expect that to always be the case as my business endeavors are starting to move in a direction that is more successful than anything I have ever known.

My point is this: the areas where I was discouraged have been the areas where I have struggled at times. The area of racing was a place in which I was never discouraged which is one of the primary reasons why I believe I experienced such tremendous success as a driver.

I bring this information to light to encourage you. Yes, some may have said you would not succeed. You may have told yourself you will not succeed. I want to tell you that all of that is incorrect. You are capable of success no matter what others have told you, you have told yourself or what you may have experienced in the past. You may be experiencing struggle right now, but God can answer the questions that will give you the answers as to how to overcome anything that is trying to overcome you!

Remember, if you can find one person who has been successful at what it is you want to do, you too can succeed. If you cannot find someone who has been successful at what it is you want to do, be the first; opening the way for others to follow you.

God created you to be a success! Why not walk in what He has for you? It does not matter how old you are, how many times you have failed or what others have said. In fact, what you have said over yourself does not matter. It is not too late to do an about face and move in the direction God has for you. Keep in mind, if you are seeking God, your desires are from Him.

"Delight yourself also in the LORD, And He shall give you the desires of your heart."

Psalm 37:4

Commonly, the words of Psalm 37:4 are interpreted to mean that God will give us what we desire if we delight ourselves in Him. Yes, God will give us what we desire such as a mate, nice home, nice vehicle, great salary and other necessities and wants of life. However, this is not the meaning of the words of Psalm 37:4.

The words, delight yourself in the Lord, literally mean, to allow your heart to become soft and pliable in His hands. When we allow our heart to be soft and pliable in the hands of God, we are allowing Him to place His desires into our hearts. For this reason, many of us have lofty goals. If your desires are greater than anything you could fulfill on your own, your desires are likely from God.

Most people settle for much less than God's best, which may come in the form of taking a low paying job because it pays the bills. God does not desire any of us to have just enough, let alone, less than enough. No wonder I dislike the mentality of our daily bread: a belief that God will always give us just enough to get through each day. No! God does not want any of us to have just enough. When a person is living on just enough, there is no opportunity to get ahead, have extra for fun, investing, emergencies or blessing and helping other people.

It is always God's plan for you to walk in a lifestyle of more than enough. God does not want you to live from paycheck to paycheck, struggling to get by and possibly having to take out a loan or refinance something to make ends meet.

I cannot tell you exactly what your experience will be to move from where you are to where God wants you to be but remember, it all begins with asking God questions and allowing Him to give you answers to those questions. You may have a job right now, but God may want you to eventually quit that job to run a business and eventually move to the third tier of income. For some, you may have a job and a business of some sort that runs itself for the most part. You may sell online and double your income without doubling the number of time invested to make a great living. Don't worry about the details.

Simply take the first, second and third step to begin moving forward as God reveals the steps to you.

As you follow God's direction, you will get out of the mess you may be in and begin to see the light at the end of the tunnel. Only this time, another train loaded with financial stress and strain will not be the source of the light!

You are capable; you are prepared. God has great plans for you. In a matter of time, you will remember what your former experience of life was like, but it will be part of the testimony you share with others of how God began turning your life right side up.

There is hope for you. You are capable!

Chapter 9
How to Move Forward Based on What You Have Read

While this book is not what some would consider being a large book to read, it is packed with a lot of information. Much of the information will challenge some readers while the information found within its pages will affirm others. How about you? What has this book done for you? What is the next step for you? Some may say, "I will ask God a question", which is a great answer! However, some will become excited and motivated for a period of time, but such emotions and experiences could fade over the next few weeks or months. I do not want this to be your experience.

What needs to change in your life right now to move from where you are to where God wants you to be? Who do you need to become today that you were not yesterday? Do you need to change the way you spend your time? Do you need to change what you are beholding? Are there habits you need to walk away from? Are there habits you need to acquire? Below are a few common habits of the wealthy. Which of these habits do you currently practice? I believe the list will shed much light on what may or may not need to change for you.

- 88 percent of the wealthy read at least 30-minutes per day.
  - 63 percent listen to audio books during daily commutes.
  - 79 percent read material related to career and occupation.
  - 55 percent read books on personal development.

- o 58 percent read biographies of successful people.
- o 94 percent read about current events.
- o 51 percent study history.
- o 11 percent read for entertainment purposes. (something to think about!)
- 63 percent spend less than an hour per day online unless it is for business related purposes.
- A high percentage of wealthy people regularly volunteer to network with others.
- Wealthy people set goals to accomplish toward fulfilling a vision as opposed to working via wishes and hopes.
- Wealthy people do not procrastinate.
- Wealthy people listen more than they speak.
- Wealthy people avoid relationships with controlling, manipulative and toxic people.

- Wealthy people don't give up.
- Wealthy people let go of beliefs that could cause them to look back to past failure in a self-limiting manner.
- Wealthy people have one or more mentors.
- Wealthy people know their purpose.
- Wealthy people can tell you about their goals and desires on the spot.
- Wealthy people know how much money they need to achieve a vision and how the money will be spent.
- Wealthy people plan ahead (are long-term minded).

- **Source – Success Magazine**

When you look over the list, which of these habits do you currently practice? Many may believe that some people are more apt to be successful than others. I highly recommend reading the biographies of those who have achieved great things in life. You may be surprised at where they come from and what they had to overcome to go from where they were to where they are. Someday it is possible that someone will read your biography and be inspired by your story of overcoming as opposed to being overcome.

I believe in you and so does God. What more could you possibly need? As long as you are confident, move ahead and start the process.

You TOO can prosper!

Conclusion

If someone were to ask you what it is that is keeping you from perusing your dreams, how would you answer? Would you have to take the time to think of an answer? A common and honest answer is a one-word answer: fear. Fear of failure, fear of success, fear of what others will think, fear of change, fear of responsibility.

No matter what the hindrance may be, I want you to ponder this question. If you knew you could move away from where you are right now and move toward what God has placed in your heart, would be willing to trade any fear of the unknown for a better life?

It is likely I do not know you or your background, but you are fully aware of your background and how your life has gone to this point.

Peter J. Daniels, once known as the richest Christian in the world, was a third-generation welfare recipient, was illiterate and worked as a bricklayer at the age of 27 when he placed his faith in Jesus Christ. He had to learn to read and think differently in all areas of his life. His life changed dramatically, but even so, he failed in business more than once before he made it. If Peter J. Daniels can prosper, you too can prosper.

Robert T. Kiyosaki grew up hearing the common advice of getting a good education, getting a safe, secure job and living in what amounts to an uncertain and limited world commonly traveled by the majority. The majority struggles financially, is stressed and unhappy with what they are doing in life. When did following the majority become the best thing to do?

In Robert's case, his best friend's dad was wealthy and understood money. Robert had to choose between his rich dad and his (biological) poor dad. He did not choose the common path and had become very wealthy while teaching others to get out of the rat race. He did so against the odds of commonality. If Robert T. Kiyosaki can prosper, you too can prosper.

My friend and mentor, Paul Milligan was raised in a low-income family by his grandparents. Based on his personal testimony, he once worked for the anti-Christ (based on experience), yet he went on to own and operate many large companies, some of which make over 100 million dollars per year. At one time in life, Paul was living in the pit of Hell on his job, yet God opened the doors and made way for him to prosper. If Paul Milligan can prosper, you too can prosper.

I personally was born legally blind. At the age of one, my parents were told that I would never live a normal life, attend regular schools, play sports or drive a car. Due to the healing power of God, I have done all of those things and more. I have failed in business more than once, yet God has brought me to a place of prosperity. If I can prosper, you too can prosper.

Based on what you have read in this book, you know where to begin the process. Ask God questions and allow Him to give you the answers, but be careful. Once He has given you an answer, begin by taking action no matter how large or small the action may be. Many take the first step of asking God and receiving guidance, but they then follow up by waiting on God. What does waiting on God look like?

Let me begin by telling you what waiting on God does not look like. Waiting on God does not look like sitting still and waiting for something to happen. You must put motion to your boat.

Waiting on God looks like expectant parents who are many months away from the birth of their child. Many months before the arrival of their child, the expectant parents are remodeling a room, painting and buying baby furniture in anticipation of what is to come. They are waiting on the birth of their child.

In the same manner, waiting on God involves taking action based on an anticipated outcome.

I encourage you to take action. Do not allow the fire that God is kindling on the inside of you to burn out. Take action today and begin moving forward because you too can prosper.

Before ending this book, I would like to pray for you. Thank you for taking the time to read. I appreciate you. God has amazing plans for you. You are a winner and a champion!

"God, I thank you for my friend who has taken the time to read this book. I thank you ahead of time for the amazing testimonies they will share over the course of time as you show them how to begin prospering or continuing to prosper beyond their wildest dreams per the words of Ephesians 3:20.

I pray that any wrong beliefs, no matter their source, will lose their grip on my friend. No matter why, I speak an end to wrong beliefs that would limit God's ability to fulfill His desires and purpose for my friend. I speak forth God-given inspiration and hope like never experienced.

I prophesy that today is the end of living in lack and the beginning of prospering according to the standards and plans of God.

I pray forth the right people to come across my friend's path to provide encouragement and guidance as they navigate their way through their new path from God. The path that leads to prosperity, unlike anything they ever thought possible.

God, I thank you ahead of time for an end to fear and anything else that would hold them back. I also thank you God for the amazing testimonies that will come over course of time from those who have read this book as they begin to fulfill their destiny from you.

I am excited about their future as I know you are too. I thank you for all of this because they are a son of God and a joint-heir with Christ. I thank for you all of this because they are the righteousness of God in Christ Jesus.

I speak all of this forth in Jesus name, amen!"

You are now free to prosper like never before. I ask that you keep me posted as you make progress.

God is on your side, and so am I!

Get in touch with Tom Tompkins.

Web – lifetimevisionary.com

Facebook facebook.com/lifetimevisionary

Twitter - twitter.com/tomtompkinsjr

Other Books Written by Tom Tompkins

Understanding The Book of Job –
Separating what is true from what is
truth

The Armor of God – Defining the
importance of knowing God's Word

The God Who Makes Sense – Defining
God's sovereignty

Avoiding Circumstantial Theology

Notes

Notes

Notes

Made in the USA
Middletown, DE
09 April 2019